# Trees *of* Bristol

# Trees *of* Bristol

PHOTOGRAPHS BY FRANK DRAKE

TEXT BY TONY D'ARPINO

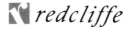 redcliffe

The authors and publishers wish to thank
the Mayor of Bristol, George Ferguson, and
Alan Stealey for their thoughtful preface
and introduction respectively; Christopher
Somerville for his generous testimonial,
and tree experts Richard Bland and Tony
Titchen for providing an effective safety net
for identifying tree species and checking
facts and figures.

First published in 2014 by Redcliffe Press Ltd., 81g Pembroke Road, Bristol BS8 3EA

www.redcliffepress.co.uk
e: info@redcliffepress.co.uk
t: 0117 9737207

© 2014 photographs Frank Drake text Tony D'Arpino
The right of Tony D'Arpino to be identified as author of this text has been asserted
in accordance with section 77 of the Copyright, Designs and Patents Act 1988

ISBN  978-1-908326-28-7

British Library Catalogue-in-Data
A catalogue record for this book is available from the British Library

Designed by Simon Bishop, Bristol
Printed and bound by Zenith Media

MIX
Paper from
responsible sources
FSC® C010353
FSC
www.fsc.org

# Preface

Frank Drake is a Bristol phenomenon – a philosopher and photographer on a strong ecological mission. In this book he brings together an acute eye for nature and the city. As an architect I recognise trees as both the antidote and friend of the built environment and we cannot overestimate their importance to our wellbeing as citizens. This book neatly coincides with the launch of my practical educational programme to double Bristol's tree canopy over a generation, involving every child in year 6 and every community, every year, until this ambitious goal is reached.

These stunningly beautiful photographs and Tony D'Arpino's rich text are a timely reminder of the importance of trees to all of us and how they become part of the structure of the city – whether planted formally or informally. Without trees there would be no birds in the city – let's listen to their song as we turn the pages…

**George Ferguson**, Mayor of Bristol

# Introduction

This publication is both beautiful and fascinating in turns. The combination of writer Tony D'Arpino and photographer Frank Drake is a force to be reckoned with.

It has been my pleasure to have known Frank for a number of years. With my responsibility for some of the locations mentioned in this book, we have spent time consuming coffee, in any one of the fantastic cafés around Clifton, talking about the trees and history of Bristol. His imagination and inspired art matches his wonderful photographs, and his encyclopaedic knowledge and memory for names and interests mean that I know of no one better for networking.

Frank introduced Tony to me last year, and I took the opportunity to show them around the Royal Fort – a former Civil War fortification now largely overlaid with a landscape designed by Humphry Repton and containing mature cork oaks (*Quercus suber*), an unusually high grafted ash (which is an indication of its age), and a fabulous mulberry (*Morus nigra*) – and other University gardens. Tony's informative, informal commentary is very rewarding to the reader. I have a real passion for local history, but the scope of this book is wonderful; ranging joyfully not only between statistics, facts, poetry and the arts but locations and cultures; creating links between Bristol and America, myth and ancient civilizations.

At all times trees remain at the heart of the narrative, strikingly illustrated with Frank's photographs taken through the seasons and throughout Bristol. As you absorb the content of the book, a central truth becomes clear – that the city is enriched by its surrounding woodland; a field enhanced by its ancient groves; and the harsh streetscape can, sometimes, be alleviated by a single tree.

For those of us who are fortunate enough to influence Bristol's rich landscape, the responsibility is profound; not only should we preserve the stock that has been passed down to us and manage its succession, whenever possible, but also plan and plant for the future. In my experience this view is encapsulated by the new University Botanic Garden (pages 30 and 31).

The Botanic Garden is the first to have been created within UK University grounds for nearly forty years. It is beautifully presented, established below mature trees – the area was formerly part of The Stoke House Estate (now known as Trinity College) – including a grove of mature oaks, two blue cedar (*Cedrus atlantica Glauca* group) and small-leaved lime (*Tilia cordata*). The garden has been filled with a huge diversity of plants, including many exotic species set in inspirational displays against the backdrop of a striking Victorian house, The Holmes, (the name meaning holly from Old English).

It has been a long-held desire for the Botanic Garden to lay out an arboriculture walk through the extended landscape, augmented with suitable trees... which could take a few decades to establish! However, as the saying goes: 'The best time to plant a tree is twenty years ago. The second best time is now.'

Many people will doubtless use this book as the inspiration to go out and explore the areas of Bristol depicted, and find a deeper understanding and appreciation for our natural heritage.

**Alan Stealey**, MSc, MCIEEM, Head of External Estates, University of Bristol

# Bristol Sylva

The trees in this book were chosen not because they are ancient or rare (though some are) but because they are the pervasive icons of our daily forest. They are the friends we meet every day, representative of every neighbourhood and district of Bristol. A book like this cannot be definitive, indeed entire books could be written on the trees of Clifton alone, as well as Bristol's ancient forest Leigh Woods.

The trees of Bristol form the continuous community of trees we see and interact with every day, whether part of a remnant forest, a council planting scheme, riverine woods, or a specimen tree. We wear the forest loosely, and often take our urban forest for granted, but we see trees every day of our lives. The woods of England are islands and each one has its own name like a village or a town. There are many forests recorded in the Domesday book of 1085. Their descendants are our closest link to the ancient wildwood which some of us still seek in our dreams and in fieldwork in real woods.

This book explores in words and images the bio-luxuriance of some of the woods and famous trees of Bristol and environs. Books are made of trees, even ebooks are ultimately sourced and powered by the carbon energy of ancient forests. All the ships in Bristol's Floating Harbour were once made of trees. Writing about trees is in a way writing about nomadics, a slow motion natural history.

> *Orpheus with his lute made trees*
> *And mountain tops that freeze*
> *Bow themselves when he did sing*
> **William Shakespeare**

Ashton Park from Clifton Wood

Trees are a part of human consciousness. They appear in all cosmographies from Assyria to Oceania. Our myths, poetry and popular culture are crowded with trees: the maypole, myths of origin, the golden bough and the secret forests of Rome, the Gothic forests of fairy tales, Sherwood Forest and Robin Hood, the forests of Tolkien, the great tree in the movie *Avatar*, the battle of the trees and the tree alphabet of Robert Graves' *The White Goddess*, and the Green Man, staring at us from his wreath of leaves, the forest speaking from his mouth and ears and eyes. The forest is endless.

Trees are shape-changers: boats, toothpicks, bookmarks, furniture, paper stacked in the printer. They can also be ghosts. Trees tell us tales of the cycles of life and the history of the landscape. They are the spiritual link between past and future, earth and sky. A bestiary of trees would include all the lichens, lice, ants, bees and beetles, fungi, all the life that fuels the green fuse of our global canopy. The tone of tree books can vary from the scientific language of forestry to the lyricism of Romantic poetry. With this book we hope to strike a local tone and share a vision of the wildwood of the everyday.

Bristol is a truly special place. There are not many cities now in which one can see hedgerows, fields, and woods from the city centre. This book is about the trees in your own neighbourhood; all the trees you know, even if you may not know all their names. It's not meant to be a handbook but a dreambook. Trees induce reverie, a kind of creative memory.

*It's always autumn in heaven*
            **John Donne**

Beech *Fraxinus excelsior*
Park Place, Clifton

# The Avon Gorge

The Avon Gorge has been botanized since humans first returned here with the new forests after the last Ice Age. That's about 12,000 years of walking in the woods. Bristol has its own epic of botany in James Walter White's magnum opus, *Flora of Bristol*. It is a scientific and poetic masterpiece and still in use as a reference book at the Bristol University Botanic Garden. White's *Flora* contains a history of local botany from the Middle Ages through the early twentieth century, from Elizabethans like William Turner and John Gerard (of *Gerard's Herbal*), to Sir Joseph Banks and others from the Age of Discovery.

Here is J W White on approaching the wooded landscape of Bristol:

> From the high ridge of Alveston Common the views extend over tracts of woodland on the lower eminences about Tockington, Elberton, and Thornbury, while the woods between Hill and Berkeley appear on the northern horizon. Nearer Bristol, beyond Henbury, are the hilly and picturesque preserves known as Haw Wood and Berwick Wood, with the tree-clad ridge of Spaniorum overlooking the Severn Sea. The woodland scenery becomes still more attractive as the city is approached, and the sylvan loveliness of the Frome Valley at Stapleton and Frenchay, of Kingsweston, Blaise Castle, and Combe Dingle, are fully appreciated by the townspeople.
>
> Crossing the river to the Somerset side we come at once to famed Leigh Woods, a fine forest-like tract that crowns the cliffs and descends to the tideway on the left bank of the Avon Gorge. These woods are the home of a plant community of uncommon interest. They contain nearly every indigenous tree in the country, and offer in consequence a foliage of singularly varied tint, from that of darkest yew to the pale light green of lime and oak, or silver of the whitebeam. The larger trees grow here on such insufficient subsoil that they sometimes put

on hues of autumn before summer is half over. The choicest part of this wide and nobly wooded space, with its Valley, Camp, and embowered ravines, beloved of Bristolians and the delight of visitors from afar, now happily belongs to the people of England.

Nearby Ashton Court Estate contains the largest single population of Veteran trees within the city with over 400 individual trees verified: 359 oaks, 31 hawthorn, 24 sweet chestnut, 11 ash, 7 field maple, 6 crack willow, and 6 other species. Veteran trees, also known as Legacy trees, are creatures of special interest because of their age, size, or nature. The Tree Register of the British Isles has researched over 200,000 of these trees. Bristol and the surrounding counties are rich in Legacy trees, in fact England as a whole has more ancient trees than all of Europe combined. There's a good reason for this amazing fact: the ancient forest practices of pollarding and coppicing.

A form of pollarding is still a common pruning practice in parks and city streets but has not been done in most woodlands for over a hundred years. Pollarding involved the pruning of the tops of trees for foliage, for animal fodder and for timber of all sizes for everything from firewood to boat building. Coppicing is the cutting of younger trees at the base to force new sapling growth. Forests and woods were coppiced every 10 to 20 years in rotation to provide a yearly harvest. Coppicing is still practised in public forests like Westonbirt Arboretum.

The iron-age settlements of Stokeleigh, Burwalls, and Clifton Camp (at the Observatory), are three of Bristol's sacred hills. There are many more hill-forts in Somerset, toward the sea and south. Most are wooded. The footpath through Nightingale Valley in Leigh Woods is an ancient holloway leading to the ancient ford on the River Avon.

There have been no nightingales in Nightingale Valley for a number of years. There are half a dozen Nightingale woods, copses, combes, and other place-names throughout the Bristol area, but the

Common Oak *(Quercus robur)*
Ashton Court Estate

nightingale population in the region has been declining for at least the past century. Tree species sometimes have similar problems, which we discuss below.

The Paddock in Leigh Woods is now tall broadleaved woodland where once horses grazed, and previous to that was a climax forest. Pruning, coppicing, pollarding are arts from the threshold of civilization. Paradise does not exist in nature, but is a man-made island. The enchantment of the landscape is the beginning of magic.

Bristol and the Avon Gorge is a truly rare landscape. From the centre of the Floating Harbour and the old city streets one can still see hedgerows, fields, and woods; a legacy of luck and planning. It wasn't that long ago that many neighbourhoods of Bristol were coalfields, another kind of ancient forest. From their deer park and big house at Ashton Court, the Smyth family in years past could watch their own dark satanic mills in operation. Today the views from Ashton Court present a very different picture, a green river-city. The views from the opposite direction, looking up the Gorge to the Suspension Bridge from Rownham Hill, or from the rise of trees near Ashton Footbridge, present another dramatic landscape of hanging woods.

> *Gardens bright with sinuous rills*
> *Where blossomed many an incense-bearing tree;*
> *And here were forests ancient as the hills,*
> *Enfolding sunny spots of greenery.*
>
> **Coleridge**, *Kubla Khan*

View from above Ashton Footbridge

# The Invisible Forest

The real forest of Avon, the ancient hunting-forest of Kingswood, once occupied a great part of the Bristol area. Royal forests were not continuous woodlands but more like the present-day New Forest (which is about the same age as Bristol's invisible forest), composed of wood pasture mixed with ancient forest stands. Kingswood extended from Sodbury to the Severn to all of Bristol and south almost to Bath. Originally created by the Saxon kings based in Pucklechurch, it was a royal wood for over a thousand years. The main timber trees were oak, ash, and giant hollies. Although there was mining from ancient times, the Bristol district known as Kingswood today was transformed into extensive coalfields in the nineteenth century, like the Bedminster and Ashton Gate neighbourhoods.

Little remains of this vast forest today, but remnant woods can be found near villages and on the banks of the River Avon in St Anne's, Hanham Woods, near the Conham Ferry at Beese's Tea Gardens, and along the River Frome from Bristol to Chipping Sodbury. 'The flexous valley of the Frome presents some charming bits of rural scenery, but the most lovely by far is on its lowest reach where, shortly before entering the city culvert, it passes by Oldbury Court and Stapleton. Glen Frome is one of the most beautiful spots in the neighbourhood of the city.'

Oldbury Court and the River Frome follow a long story from Saxon forest to medieval hunting lodge, from Elizabethan manor house to mills, to the urban park we know today. The 25-mile Frome Valley Walkway begins near Castle Park and leads into the Cotswolds beyond Chipping Sodbury. The riverine woods of the Frome and the Avon are a vast accessible ancient forest relict, riverrun indeed.

There are some beautiful riverine willows in Bristol but wild willows have their own life on the network of rhynes in the local levels and saltmarshes along the Severn estuary. There is an ancient road made of willow in the Somerset Levels called the Sweet Track. It

Sweet Chestnut *Castanea sativa*
Blaise Castle

is named after Mr Sweet who discovered it many centuries after it was built. The Sweet Track has been dated by dendrochronology, tree-ring analysis, to 3800 BC. Crack willow (*Salix fragilis*) is also common in the wet meadows and hedgerows of Lawrence Weston Moor.

Some of the landscape White describes has not changed too much in 100 years. The suburbs have swallowed many villages, woods, farms, and orchards, but ancient forest remnants survive in other nearby woods such as Priory Woods at Portbury, the woods in Wraxall and Tickenham Hills, as well as the extensive range of primitive limestone woods that still stretches almost continuously from Backwell Hill to Congresbury and Wrington.

Woodland shrub-layer trees are often overlooked, but they are beautiful citizens: wayfaring tree (*Viburnum lantana*), guelder rose (*Viburnum opulus*), buckthorn (*Rhamnusca thartica*), spindle (*Euonymus europaeus*), wild privet (*Ligustrum vulgare*), and tree cotoneaster (*Cotoneaster frigidus*). Ancient forest understory sounds like a ritual incantation: dog's mercury, daffodil, fly orchid, meadow saffron, bluebell, wood sorrel, herb paris (true lover's knot), and pyramidal orchid.

Spring brings out the elders of Bedminster, the great white wheels of dreaming elderflower. In deep summer the alleys of Clifton are drowsy with the hanging buddleia of garden walls. Urban forest understory also includes traveller's joy and red valerian. For me the climax of the forest year is seeing the trees of summer swimming in the sky.

Magnolia (*Magnolia x soulangeana*)
Clifton

*Nature is a temple where living pillars*
*Sometimes let out confused words.*
*Man passes there through a forest of symbols*
*Which observe him with a familiar gaze*

**Charles Baudelaire**

A magnificent tree canopy in its traffic-congested location
London Plane *(Platanus x hybrida)*
Whiteladies Road

# A Grove Within the Forest

'The oak bears more things besides its fruit than any other tree'
**Theophrastus** 300 BC

The ancient Druids are one of the most mysterious of forest folk. The actual historical writings about them are positively Shakespearean in their brevity and scarceness, almost all from the first century CE. Julius Caesar's mention of them is the most famous but Suetonius, Pliny, Strabo, Tacitus, the Roman poet Lucan, and others have all contributed legends and conflicting reports. The Latin light does not pierce the forest mists. The modern Druids of course are very visible, especially in the West Country, but their cult originates in the late 1700s with the visionary Welsh poet Iolo Morganwg (Edward Williams), who has a connection with Bristol (and with the work of Thomas Chatterton) through his friendship with the Romantic poets Samuel T Coleridge and Robert Southey. Morganwg's father was a stone mason and they both may have worked on projects at St Mary Redcliffe church.

There is a fascinating book by University of Bristol historian Ronald Hutton called *Blood and Mistletoe: The History of the Druids in Britain*. Prof Hutton surveys the extant ancient Druidic literature and their lore and history to the present day, a definitive and graceful work. The Druids still walk among us.

The sacred trees of the Druids are generally easy to identify as 'oaks', but on close inspection they are as individual as humans and could have their own horoscopes. Oaks readily and happily hybridize. Our two native oaks are the English oak (*Quercus robur*) known as pedunculate, with stalked acorn cups, and the sessile oak (*Quercus petraea*) or durmast oak with stalkless acorn cups.

Durmast has a definite preference for rocky places but can be found anywhere. Oaks can easily live 300 to 500 years, but pollarded oaks can be over a thousand years old.

The holm oak (*Quercus ilex*), also known as holly oak and evergreen oak, is indeed an evergreen with leaves often similar to the olive. It was introduced into England around 1580. It is so popular

*I frequently tramped eight or ten miles through the deepest snow to keep an appointment with a beech-tree, or a yellow birch, or an old acquaintance among the pines.*

**Henry David Thoreau**

Oak leaves *(Quercus robur)*

and prolific in Bristol that some neighbourhoods like Clifton Village and Cliftonwood can almost be considered an urban holm oak forest. Another import, the Turkey oak (*Quercus cerris*) can be identified by its acorns with the curly bristles.

There are 736 named oak trees in England. The famous oak of Sherwood Forest, called the Major Oak, over 1,000 years old, was a sapling in Robin Hood's time. Bristol's own ancient, The Domesday Oak, is sadly only a third of its former size due to recent storms. Outlaw jays are still hiding golden acorns and over the centuries have produced much forest. One mature oak in a good mast year can produce 50,000 acorns. The ancient right of pannage, by which commoners could let their animals forage in the woods, is still practised in the New Forest where the famous ponies make way for the local pigs hoovering acorns and beechnuts. Similar rights also still exist in the Forest of Dean. Bristol's Leigh Woods has recently reintroduced Red Devon cattle in Stokeleigh Camp to keep the archaeological sites from becoming overgrown, and goats have been added to Gully Quarry on Durdham Down to curb invasive undergrowth.

Oak lore is itself prolific. In the Welsh epic *The Mabinogion* a girl is conjured from the flowers of an oak. In late summer, around Lammas Day (August 1), oaks produce what is known as Lammas shoots. These leafy new growths make all the great oaks in a forest stand out with a bright new green glow in the dog-days of late summer and first harvest. Mistletoe (*Viscum album*), a partial parasite of oak, silver birch, and many other trees, is one of our more ancient forest talismans, emblematic of seasonal tree-magic.

John Evelyn, author of *Sylva* in 1664, wrote of oak as England's 'wooden walls', a reference to the classic age of shipbuilding. The herbalist Nicholas Culpeper doesn't bother to describe oak at all in his famous herbal, stating it's too well known, all English people know the oak. Most people also know that oakwood barrels are used to enhance the aroma and flavour of Scotch whisky, traditionally made from old sherry casks from Portugal and Spain. Oak bourbon casks from the southern United States are also used now, but there seems to be an unending need for new barrels as well.

Holm oak *(Quercus ilex)*
Pembroke Road

27

Common oak *(Quercus Robur)*
Clarken Coombe, Ashton Court Estate

The poet Walt Whitman, author of *Leaves of Grass*, wrote a book titled *Specimen Days* which has this story-dream about an oak.

## Thoughts under an oak – a dream

June 2. – This is the fourth day of a dark northeast storm, wind and rain. Day before yesterday was my birthday. I have now enter'd on my 60th year. Every day of the storm, protected by overshoes and a waterproof blanket, I regularly come down to the pond, and ensconce myself under the lee of the great oak; I am here now writing these lines. The dark smoke-color'd clouds roll in furious silence athwart the sky; the soft green leaves dangle all round me; the wind steadily keeps up its hoarse, soothing music over my head – Nature's mighty whisper. Seated here in solitude I have been musing over my life – connecting events, dates, as links of a chain, neither sadly nor cheerily, but somehow, to-day here under the oak, in the rain, in an unusually matter-of-fact spirit.

My great oak – sturdy, vital, green – five feet thick at the butt. I sit a great deal near or under him. Then the tulip tree near by – the Apollo of the woods – tall and graceful, yet robust and sinewy, inimitable in hang of foliage and throwing-out of limb; as if the beauteous, vital, leafy creature could walk, if it only would. (I had a sort of dream-trance the other day, in which I saw my favourite trees step out and promenade up, down and around, very curiously – with a whisper from one, leaning down as he pass'd me, *We do all this on the present occasion, exceptionally, just for you.*)

**Walt Whitman** *Specimen Days*

Local oaks have always been important as boundary trees and landmarks. In Norman times a court was set up to deal summarily with thieves and debtors of the Bristol Fair which took place in Old Market, outside the Postern Gate of Bristol Castle, called the Pie-Poudre Court (also spelt *pie poudre* or Piepowders). The name comes from the French, 'pieds poudrés' which can be translated as 'dusty

feet', and was a temporary court set up for the duration of the fair to deal with travellers who were not resident in the town. It was held in the open air under an ancient oak, now the site of the Stag and Hounds public house.

There is a Lucombe Oak near the Observatory on Clifton Down, which is a hybrid between the Cork Oak and the Turkey Oak. It was first propagated by Exeter nurseryman William Lucombe in the 1760s and is an unusual specimen tree but not uncommon in gardens of the West Country. It is said that Mr. Lucombe was so impressed with the timber, that he kept planks of it under his bed to make his coffin.

In *Flora of Bristol*, J W White identifies a Bristol oak of very unusual size and age . . . in the grounds of The Holmes in Stoke Bishop. The remnant of this tree still stands there at the magnificent old estate, now the site of the University of Bristol Botanic Garden. The Botanic Garden has moved a number of times over the past 130 years, leaving a legacy of other-worldly gardens and specimen trees across the city. Its current home near the edge of Durdham Down is a kind of Shangri-la, with exotic tree specimens and the latest hybrid research, in what seems to be its own unique micro-climate.

The University of Bristol's Biological Sciences Department buildings now occupy the site of Bristol's first Botanic Garden. A ginkgo and a magnolia tree (unfortunately now in decline) are still in the grounds. Another former botanic garden site in the grounds of Senate House still has a lovely Pagoda tree (*Sophora japonica*), a Chinese ash grafted onto an English ash, and a Kentucky coffee tree (*Gymnocladus dioicus*). The legacy of the garden's most recent site at Bracken Hill, adjacent to Leigh Woods, continues to evolve. Now privately owned, the site contains a true exotica of trees, Atlas cedar, Lawson cypress, a large mimosa and a huge Chilean firetree, holm oaks, camellias, and rhododendrons.

The Bristol University External Estates Department manages a number of local legacy estates and gardens with significant plantings. Goldney Gardens with its apple orchard is rightly the most famous, but the grounds of Hampton House, the old Homeopathic Hospital, has fine oaks and yews and a great Tree of Heaven. For espaliers and

*How sweet it is, when mother Fancy rocks*
*The wayside brain, to saunter through a wood!*
**William Wordsworth**

Medlar *(Mespilus germanica)*
University of Bristol Botanic Garden,
Stoke Bishop

Bristol's famous pergola, sometimes referred to as 'Birdcage Walk', running through the old cemetery of former St Andrews Church, Clifton, blitzed in the war. Common Lime (*Tilia x europaea*)

pergolas there's nothing like attending Open Days at some of the secret gardens of Bristol. Bristol's most famous pergola, Birdcage Walk, is open to the public year-round. It is a shady tree-tunnel through the old churchyard of St Andrew's Church, which was lost in the Blitz. The urban forest has invaded this churchyard and now includes some rare specimen trees. A woodland has also overtaken parts of Bristol's much larger Arnos Vale cemetery.

# The Forest of Symbols

*The inside of the temple will be like a forest*

**Antoni Gaudi**

The film director Peter Bogdanovich in his *Year and A Day* tree-calendar book quotes from the poem 'The Owl and The Pussycat' by Edward Lear to make a point about how trees are deeply embedded in human consciousness:

> They sailed away, for a year and a day,
> To the land where the Bong-tree grows.

'Nonsense verse, we're told. Yet if we happen to learn that the Owl was the totem-bird for variously named goddesses of wisdom, and that the Cat was the totem-animal for variously named Cat-goddesses . . . and that both a year and day, and the land of the Bong-tree, resonate with references to an ancient tree-calendar, the poem suddenly makes a different kind of sense.' There is a local connection to 'The Owl and The Pussycat'. The poem was written by Lear for the young daughter of Bristol writer John Addington Symonds while they lived at Clifton Hill House.

Like trees hidden in a forest, Robert Graves' tree-alphabet poem from his book *The White Goddess* was hidden in another poem called 'The Battle of the Trees'. Tree lore as hidden knowledge. As Richard Mabey says, 'The idea that ordinary woods may have been

flourishing for perhaps 10,000 years, is something we have only just begun to comprehend.' And then there's the fact of the diageotropic nature of roots and branches: the natural tendency of trees to grow at right angles to the line of gravity. Nearly as surprising as the fact that Bedminster was once covered in ancient forest. Sacred trees and sacred wells are still part of our enchanted landscape. We still meet in the woods in the night before May Day.

# Primeval

Lucky is the child who has access to a magic forest. I can trace my love of trees to the town where I was born. Mount Holly, New Jersey is a green colonial town of creeks, trees and secret forests. In colonial days it was called Bridgetown. The eponymous Mount still has many holly trees, as well as beech, oak, ash, pine, and sycamore (called buttonwood locally), and indigenous North American species like hickory and sassafras (which first came to Bristol in 1602). My old woods have the American excess of oaks: white oak, post oak, pin oak, black oak, northern red oak, scarlet oak, chestnut oak, to name a few. The local woods became my green world. A flowering dogwood was my first treehouse, but the real forest was just a street and alley away. Most of this forest was on an island accessible only by railway trestles. A secret forest at the end of the mind.

The temperate zone is a misnomer of some magnitude, with its seasons of dramatic extremes: almost tropical summers and nearly nordic winters. The West Country is more mild and spring seems to come earlier. The English spring is announced by mays, primrose, daffodils and snow-drops, and the vast under-forest cloudscapes of bluebells.

There are many trees in my primeval memory theatre. Some from the forested slopes of The Big Island of Hawai'i where I managed a private forest reserve in deep south Kona. That is indeed another story, but I carry a tropical sylva of 'Ohi'a lehua, mamaki, sandlewood, and koa trees, as if I were an outrigger canoe.

For many years I lived in California, home of the giant sequoias, the planet's largest living things, and their taller but less massive relatives, the coast redwoods. Neither tree grows as tall in England as in their native habitat but they are widely planted here. The old Burwalls estate, built on the site of the stone-age settlement near the Leigh Woods anchor of Clifton Suspension Bridge, has a number of mature sequoias. Bristol's tallest building, St Mary Redcliffe, at 292 feet, is nearly the size these redwoods attain in their natural habitats.

I also lived for a time in Oregon where I traced the route of the great Scottish explorer and field botanist David Douglas. In the 1820s Douglas discovered in the American Northwest and Hawai'i many trees and plants we're now very familiar with: the musk-scented monkey-flower (which has lost its scent), red-flowering currant, California poppy, and many others.

David Douglas sent the seeds of the tree now named after him to his brother, who was Clerk of the Works at Drumlanrig Castle. The tree was planted out in 1832 and is now over 20 feet in girth. Douglas fir is an uncommon if beautiful sight in Bristol suburbs and old estates. Other trees introduced by Douglas include the sugar pine (*Pinus lamber-tiana*), grand fir (*Abies grandis*), Noble fir (*Abies procera*), and Sitka spruce (*Picea sitchensis*), now the monoculture species of forestry plantations.

There are many Kama'aina trees in Bristol, to use the Hawai'ian term meaning 'been here so long you're family.' It surely started long before the Romans, both our chestnuts, the holm oak, the mulberry, ginkgo, and others are now naturalised in English woodlands. John Tradescant the Younger by 1656 already had North American trees growing in his London gardens. John Bartram, the Philadelphia botanist, sent hundreds of new species to Europe in the mid-1700s.

The ginkgo (*Ginkgo biloba*) is a deciduous tree originally from Asia that is now a common street and garden tree in most cities of the world owing to its resistance to urban air pollution. Its name is from the Chinese and Japanese ideogram meaning 'silver fruit'. The ginkgo is so ancient that its system of leaf veins predates those found in any other living tree. A true living fossil unchanged for 200 million years. There are massive 1000 year-old specimen trees in South Korea.

Araucaria, the monkey puzzle tree, is the Chilean pine (*Araucaria araucana*), related to the Norfolk Island pine, and the similar Cook's pine which is endemic to the island of Lana'i in Hawai'i. Like the

Brandon Hill

Arnos Vale cemetery

ginkgo and the horsetails from our allotments, the Araucaria is an archetype tree from the days of the dinosaurs.

Other tree talismans (not all mine) include an Osage orange from childhood; a grove of Australian ironwood trees on the beach at Haleiwa on the northshore of O'ahu; a great living hollow oak at Whitcombe Farm near Beaminster, Dorset; a grove of whitebeam in Leigh Woods overlooking Nightingale Valley; a climbable Cedar of Lebanon at Frensham Heights School in Surrey; a great mulberry in Victoria Square, Clifton; and many holly trees (*Ilex aquifolium*) on many islands. On the outskirts of Bristol are the relics of the miles-long holly hedges of the old estates of Wheatground and Tyntesfield.

*Tree! Rising! O pure transcendence!*
*Orpheus sings! O great tree of sound!*

**Rainer Maria Rilke**

## A Season of Neighbourhoods

In a poem by the American poet W S Merwin, the narrator-poet observes that his parents didn't know the names of the trees in their street. We all know oaks and daffodils, beech and bluebells, pine and snowdrops, but there are over 40 species of trees in Bristol and hundreds of other plants. We may not know them personally, but they are fellow citizens of the urban forest.

There are no trees in my street, which is fairly rare in Bristol. Some Victorian terraces do have very narrow pavements. But I have many local trees also in my portable forest, a kind of botanist's vasculum. Instead of specimen trees I like to think of them as character trees, as they all have a strong character, either in their own presence or in their situation in the hyper-urban world around them. My short list includes a noble beech with a great magpie nest in the front garden of the rectory of St Francis Church near the Tobacco Factory in Southville (a tour of trees is often accompanied by birds); the fig trees on the harbour at Castle Park, near the grain barge with its ballast seed garden; a sentinel oak on the hedgerow of our allotment; a ginkgo at an artist's cottage on Wild Country Road on the edge of Long Ashton; a willow on the floating river near the shot tower; a grove of black poplars on the New Cut in front of the brick tobacco warehouse now the Bristol Record Office; and a row of Japanese maples at Temple Circus Gyratory.

Monkey puzzle tree or Chilean pine
*(Araucaria araucaria)*
Clifton Down

41

Dawn Redwood
*(Metasequoia glyptostroboides)*
University of Bristol

Common Yew *(Taxus baccata)* at Bristol's leaning tower of Temple Church

Beech (*Fagus sylvatica*) is the poem-tree of the forest on whose vellum bark lovers' names and poems have been inscribed, circling the bark for centuries, disappearing into unreadable cuneiform as the tree grows and ages. The great grey beech-claws of the local forests are welcoming as well as foreboding, depending on the play of light. The snowdrops (*Galanthus nivalis*) beneath the elephant skin avenues of beech in Barrow Gurney, noted in White's *Flora*, are still there, as are the nearby beechwoods of the old asylum.

There is a great copper beech in the communal garden of Cornwallis Crescent and there are many others throughout Bristol. Well-planted and well-loved, the copper beech is rarely ever copper-coloured, a more reddish wine-dark patina its normal range.

Durdham Down was still a wild place just 100 years ago. Whether owned by the Society of Merchant Venturers or the highwaymen, Durdham Down first appears in history in an Anglo-Saxon document in 883. Its prehistory and natural beauty are what we love about it. A dangerous and delicate place with its own famous trees and stories. The Seven Sisters group of Austrian pine trees (*Pinus nigra*) are now reduced to three, but the latest urban myth says seven saplings are doing well not far away. The White Tree of Bristol has changed shape and even species over the years.

Straight through the centre of Durdham Down is the Roman Road which went from Portus Abonae (Sea Mills) to Aqua Sulis (Bath). Outside of a few villas and settlements like Long Ashton and Wrington, the city of Bristol would not exist for another 900 years. In the old days the only trees on the Downs were hawthorns, but since the sheep have left the ash trees, elder, ivy and other natives have begun to dominate. A gibbet once stood in Gallows Acre Lane, now Pembroke Road.

Greville Smyth Park in Southville, the site of an old estate called Clift House, is a sloping cornucopia of specimen trees. North American Indian bean tree (*Catalpa bignonioides*), Cedar of Lebanon, weeping ash, silver birch, firs and pines, oaks and plane trees, and vast avenues of lime. My favourite is the triple-trunked giant sequoia (*Sequoiadendron giganteum*) sometimes called Wellingtonia in England. It has a heritage sapling a few hundred feet away. There's

also a deodar (*Cedrus deodara*) from the great rhododendron forests of the Himalayas.

There are islands of pine in any tree tour. Scots pine (*Pinus sylvestris*) is our only true endemic pine and can live 250 years. Scots pine were the old drove-road markers. Pine waymarking, 'pine-ways', were common along the Welsh borders and in the southern chalk downs, here and in Wiltshire and Dorset. Norway spruce (*Picea abies*) has been the English Christmas tree since Victorian times, but the Yule-tide decoration of trees is an ancient festival of prehistoric origin.

Pines and conifers are the psychedelic painters of the tree world, ranging from blue to yellow and every green in-between, they rival the autumn colours of their deciduous cousins. But perhaps the greatest artist of the trees with its bark overlapping in a three-dimensional puzzle, is the London plane tree (*Platanus x hispanica*). It is actually more characteristic of Paris than London, but Bristol is proud of her many planes. There are 60 mature plane trees about 150 years old in Queen Square, with 10 younger specimens planted in 2000. The beautiful plane trees on Narrow Quay and elsewhere on Bristol's Harbourside are the result of a national tree-planting scheme implemented by the Bristol Civic Society. In historical times of course there were no trees on Bristol docks, when Narrow Quay was described as a street full of ships and a forest of masts.

Bristol's many parks, cemeteries and green belts, are high-quality urban woodland. Many of our place names are evocative of groves and forests past, some imaginary. Withywood never had willows. Nine Tree Hill has no trees today but leads to a most poetic Fremantle Square with a fine hawthorn and yew. The Caucasian wingnut tree (*Pterocarya fraxinifolia*) from the walnut family can be seen in a stately colonnade along the floating river just behind Temple Meads railway station and in some large specimens on and near the Downs.

There is a spectacular Cedar of Lebanon in the churchyard of Long Ashton where the parents of Bristol poet Robert Southey are buried. The vale of Long Ashton has many Cedars of Lebanon, remnants of old estate specimen tree plantings. Medlars (*Mespilus germanica*) are rare but native. They were elusive to our own Mr White, though he found one on the undercliff at Clevedon in 1879, 'still there, 1906, in

*The hearts of plants*
*I understand*
*The stillness above the sky*
*But never the words of men*
*Trees were my teachers*
*Melodious trees*
*Down the wind*
*Go the words*

**Hölderlin**

Tree on right foreground is a deodar
(*Cedrus deodara*), the Himalayan cedar.
Greville Smyth Park

good state. Only a single tree, but growing in a situation where it certainly was never planted. Another tree, which I have not seen, is reported
from the Nightingale Valley Woods, near Weston-in-Gordano.'

Sweet chestnut (*Castanea sativa*), another Kama'aina tree, was
introduced to Britain by the Romans, who seem to have brought it from
Asia Minor and planted it everywhere. 'It is a curious fact that in every
European language the name is similar in sound; and, like the botanical
name, was apparently derived from the town of Castanea in Thessaly.'
The venerable chestnut in Tortworth Park in Gloucestershire is justly
celebrated. John Claudius Loudon, in his *Arboretum Britannicum*,
writes: 'The old Chestnut at Tortworth may possibly have been one of
those planted by the Romans. It is mentioned as a farmer's or boundary
tree in King John's time, and is stated to have been so remarkable for its
magnitude in the reign of King Stephen (1135), as then to be called the Great
Chestnut of Tortworth.' This worthy ancient tree is said to have last borne
fruit in 1788. Today nothing remains of the original trunk but decayed
wood, among which are new boles filled every summer with rich foliage.

'The oldest trees I have met with near the city are in the Old Park between Abbots Leigh and Failand, and at the north end of Frenchay Common. There are several handsome ones of fair size in Leigh Woods near the
Avon.' There's a 300-year-old chestnut in the grounds of the old Chester-
field Hospital in Clifton and many more in the surrounding countryside.

Wild cherry (*Prunus Avium*) is abundant in Leigh Woods, in the
woods between Stoke Bishop and Sea Mills, and in St. Anne's Wood,
Brislington. From White: 'A curious report reached me during the
last week of 1900 – that the cherry trees in Stoke Bishop were in
flower! Up to that date there had been no frost. It turned out that
the deceptive appearance of silvery Clematis fruit trailing among the
branches had deluded some superficial observer.'

In Henleaze the 800-year-old Phoenix hedgerow was discovered 20
years ago by local botanist Sylvia Kelly.

Silver Lime (*Tilia tomentosa*)
Fremantle Square, Kingsdown

A solitary tree on Stokes Croft stands next
to graffiti that quotes Albert Camus

Kingsdown

Above: Lime trees *(Tilia)*
Temple Park

Opposite: Bee Tree *(Euodia hupehensis)*
Kingsdown

Above: Green Man carvings in St Mary Redcliffe.

Opposite: A couple celebrate the spirit of the Green Man at a local music festival.

# The Green Man

There is a Green Man in Bristol. He is the spirit of the old forest. There are Green Women too. The Green Man's consort is the Earth Goddess, known by the many names of our grandmothers, Gaia, Astarte, Sheela-na-gig, the White Goddess. On a pagan hill above the River Avon, St Mary Redcliffe church, unarguably the loveliest parish church in England, has dozens of green men. Jacks in the green and foliate masks entwine the doors of the famous north porch, as Pevsner noted, figures hidden in a jungle of flowers. There are Green Man roof bosses in the transept and nave, a corbel holding John Cabot's whale rib beneath the tower, and a Green Man stained-glass window in the American Chapel. There is also a Green Man on the misericord in the choir of Bristol Cathedral, and on the armrests of the choir stalls in St Mark's, the so-called Lord Mayor's Chapel on College Green.

The Green Man is deep image cosmography and ranges from the pre-Islamic Al Khidr, the Verdant One, to Cernunnos, the horned god, to the Green Lion of Alchemy and the iconography of the Gothic cathedrals. We know the names of some of the old woodland gods from the Pillar of the Boatmen, a preserved bas-relief pillar from a temple of ancient Lutetia (modern Paris) from a time when the Gaulish gods and the Roman gods began to mix. It's still in Paris on exhibit at the Musée de Cluny. These are the green vegetation gods Cernunnos, Esus, and the Bull with Three Cranes.

The Green Man is the archetype of death and renewal. In *Sir Gawain and the Green Knight*, the Arthurian legends twine like ivy around our green fingerprints and seasonal quests. Photosynthesis, the process by which plants convert sunlight to sugars and growth, mirrors our lungs of branching trees. Chlorophyll Man.

# First the Forests

The city was once the forest. Our origins are of people of the forest. The Romans too were originally forest folk. In his book *The New Science*, the Italian writer Giambattista Vico, describes the order of human institutions, 'First the forests, after that the huts, then the villages, next the cities, and finally the academies.' Vico is primarily known for his cyclic theory of history but also for his meditations on the ancient forest as both the origin and the enemy of civilization.

Humans first made clearings in the forest in order to see the gods or to perform the auspices of divination. Vico says the first Roman clearing was made by Vulcan in order to see the direction from which Zeus sent his thunderbolts. According to Vico words themselves are fables and etymology is a form of creative archaeology. Likewise the subtitle of Robert Graves' *The White Goddess* is 'a historical grammar of poetic myth'.

> These woodland places
> Once the homes of local fauns and nymphs
> Together with a race of men that came
> From tree trunks, from hard oak
> **Virgil**, *Aeneid*

Rome was born of the forests and was later reclaimed by them. In the Dark Ages the Roman Forum became a wild pasture for local cattle and the old Roman roads were lost in wilderness. Not only did Rome leave England, Rome left Rome.

Like Rome's Romulus and Remus, Bristol too has its legendary founders, Brennus and Belinus. A proper city, founded on a river in a forest. The cities of prehistory are still with us and they provoke a nostalgia for the wooden world. Vico explains how the classical cultures of Greece and Rome became sky-worshippers and the far older tree-worshipper cultures and the forests themselves became things to be feared.

The language of enchantment is pervasive, we speak of family trees, the tree of life, a memory tree, or a bearing tree. The forest in

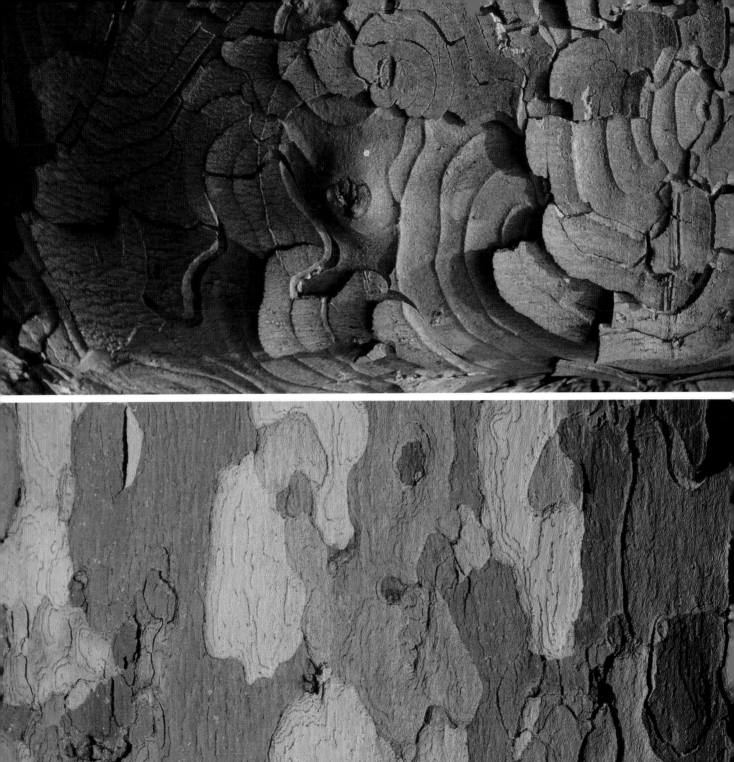

Above: Apples *(Malus domestica)*
at Goldney Hall, Clifton

Opposite: Red Horse Chestnut *(Aesculus x carnea)*
Abbots Leigh

*Copses in grey-red or grey-yellow – the tinges immediately forerunning the opening of full leaf. Meadows skirting Seven-Bridge road voluptuous green. Some oaks are out in small leaf. Ashes not out, only tufted with their fringy blooms. Hedges springing richly. Elms in small leaf, with more or less opacity. White poplars most beautiful in small grey crisp spray-like leaf. Cowslips capriciously colouring meadows in creamy drifts.*

**Gerard Manley Hopkins,** Diary 1866

the cultural imagination of the west is both sacred and profane. In the ancient Sumerian epic of *Gilgamesh*, the forest is a central image. Gilgamesh was a real king of the Sumerian city of Uruk around 2700 BC. The epic describes a forest journey, a duel with a forest guardian, the demon Huwawa, and ultimately the destruction of a cedar forest.

# Pome poems

Saxon Brigstowe, the Place of the Bridge, Bridgetown, was built of wood, as was the bridge itself and the first motte-and-bailey fort. By Norman times Bristol was a double city, town and castle. North of the old city were the monastery orchards, seeds of contemplation. These were the abbeys and monasteries that made the West Country a great library of apples.

Apple trees are almost human and have a human lifespan of about 80 years. (Pears, however, can live for 300 years.) Bristol at one time had apple orchards everywhere from the slope of Clifton Vale down to the marsh, all over St Pauls and Stokes Croft and out into the country. To get to the ancient St James' Fair one took the lanes through apple orchards of St James' Priory. Of this greenbelt of twelfth-century apple orchards there are only remnants. There's a heritage orchard at Goldney Garden managed by the Bristol Botanic Gardens with re-established specimens that replicate some of the Goldney family's vast seventeenth- and eighteenth-century fruit plantings.

A contemporary specimen collection commemorates the Long Ashton Research Station, a now vanished landmark of cider-making and fruit science, an important part of the agricultural history of Bristol. For a hundred years the orchards and fields south of Long Ashton were the home of a series of world-famous research institutes and laboratories.

The American nurseryman John Chapman, known as Johnny Appleseed, was a zealot of cider, planting thousands of trees throughout Pennsylvania, Ohio, and the Midwest. Johnny Appleseed grew apple trees from seed, not grafted. As every cider house knows, apples don't grow true from seed, but new hybrids are sometimes

Giant Sequoia or Wellingtonia
(*Sequoiadendron giganteum*)
The Mansion House, Clifton

discovered. A Somerset cider maker has a line in its recent advertising: To be an apple there's no greater honour.

Apple Wassail, the ancient singing to the orchards, a time of great good will, still happens here in the West Country on 'Old Twelvey Night' (17 January). Orchard-visiting, the singing-awake of the apples, is an ancient rite of winter in the cyder-producing counties. Wassail was a religious event long before the celebration of Christmas began in the third century. Robert Frost's poem about a cow drunk on windfall apples is clearly from his time in Dymock, Gloucestershire with the cyder-drinking Dymock Poets who included Edward Thomas, Rupert Brooke, Lascelles Abercrombie and Wilfrid Gibson.

Wassail bowls are traditionally made of white maple. Wassail is still observed in Bristol and environs, in Clevedon and Hewish, near Weston-super-Mare, and in Street and Carhampton in south Somerset, among others. Wassail is a blessing of the winter stars. As Rilke says, 'Dare to speak what you call apple.'

## The Art of Trees

Forests appear in all the arts and speak most eloquently to the visual imagination. Think of the trees of William Blake, John Constable, Thomas Gainsborough, Paul Nash and David Hockney. Arthur Rackham's illustrations for *Grimm's Fairy Tales* often feature coppiced and pollarded forest trees. One of Gustave Doré's illustrations for the *Divine Comedy* shows Dante at the foot of a huge tree in a dark Gothic forest. In Blake's engraving Virgil and Dante wander a similar haunted forest. The elmy paintings and drawings of Constable, more a tree-dreamer than Turner, the cloud-dreamer, who did paint the Avon Gorge.

Many artists have painted the Avon Gorge over the centuries. Francis Danby, a painter of the Bristol School of the Romantic era, is one of the finest with many views of Leigh Woods and the Gorge. Although harbour scenes may predominate in Bristol paintings, there are striking woodland scenes by Thomas Rowbotham, Samuel Jackson, James Johnson, and Samuel Hieronymous Grimm, among

Common Oak
Clifton Down

Copper beech *(Fagus sylvatica f. purpurea)*
Clifton Down

Nightingale Valley.
Species include Cherry, Small-leaved Lime,
Ash, Whitebeam, Sycamore.

others. There are many rainbows. John Lavars' *Balloon View of Avonmouth Bristol* and his breathtaking panorama *Bird's Eye View of Bristol* from the late 1800s are two of the more famous lithographs.

Contemporary Bristol artists have celebrated the Avon Gorge. The lush woodcuts of Trevor Haddrell feature the bridges and forests of Bristol and the work of Richard Long contains not only the wood of the forests but the very mud of the famous pils of the River Avon. I can say from experience, the view from a hot-air balloon of the woods and forests of the Bristol area is an almost four-dimensional tactile, visceral experience.

It's easy on entering Leigh Woods, to be transported into the Ballad of Robin Hood or into the Forest of Arden from *As You Like It*. The human mind is a kind of forest and a kind of theatre.

The music of the forest is seductive as well as healing. Bristol songwriter Patrick Duff (formerly lead singer of the group Strangelove) has spoken of his transformative experiences in Leigh Woods. Trance tracks lead into the shaman woods. Yes, music and theatre and oracles happen in Leigh Woods. The trees sang for Orpheus and the trees sing to each other in pheromones. Music, that mysterious form of time, is endemic to the forest and includes the sounds of a cello, viola, violin, double bass, sitar, sarod, lute, mandolin, ukelele, Aeolian harp.

One man's forest is another's art form. John Constable's iconic pencil and wash drawing *Elms in Old Hall Park* looks like a sepia photograph. Some writers on woodlands have noted the difficulties in photographing trees, especially within a forest. One thinks of a forest as naturally photogenic, but with a camera lens one is immediately confronted with the cosmography of contrasts, light and shadow morphing with the wind in the trees. The difficulty of getting the proper dose of luminosity is compounded by a geometrical difficulty. Shadow speaks of light by indicating where the light comes from.

Forest protection is a world canopy issue. The redwood forest battles in northern California and the Pacific Northwest were widely reported in the 1990s at the same time as the road protest movement in England was happening. Hundreds of people moved into the forests, living in tents, huts and tree houses to protect the destruction of ancient woodlands. Solesbury Hill near Bath was a major protest site but the most famous

was probably the Newbury bypass, a nine-mile stretch of the A34. Fierce opposition included a march of over 5,000 people and the building of 20 tree villages to save a woodland. In the end the road-work felled more than 10,000 mature forest trees. The struggle continues. The recent return of road protests near Hastings, because of a road bypass through beautiful woodland, will be another Battle of the Trees.

Protection of the great tropical forests is ongoing. The rate of forest destruction is decidedly grim but there are lights in the forest. The group Instituto Terra, founded by Brazilian photographer Sebastião Salgado, have planted 500,000 trees in the Atlantic Forest, the great but ravaged woodland of north-east Brazil.

Road construction, like agriculture, is an invasive, anti-ecological technology. Motorways are the monomaniacs of landscape. England can seem like one big roundabout sometimes, but there are green amenities. The copses and groves in the larger roundabouts are now mature woodlands.

William Blake said some see a tree as just a green thing in the way. Anyone reading this book is probably going to think otherwise. Planting a tree creates a wooden credit card which can be spent in eternity.

We sought the hollow ash that was shelter from the rain
With our pockets full of peas we had stolen from the grain
How delicious was the dinner time on such a showry day
O words are poor receipts for what time hath stole away
The ancient pulpit trees and the play

**John Clare**

Hornbeam *(Carpinus betulus)*
Abbots Leigh

Ancient yew *(Taxus baccata)*
Holy Trinity churchyard, Abbots Leigh

# Yew

*From the deep fissures of the naked rock*
*The yew-tree bursts! Beneath its dark green boughs*
*Where broad smooth stones jut out in mossy seats,*
*I rest*

**Samuel T Coleridge**
'Lines composed while climbing the left ascent of Brockley Combe, 1795'

Bristol International Airport now lies on the plateau to the east of Brockley Combe, a large wooded area of remnant woods and forestry plantations. To the southwest is the more wild forest of Goblin Combe. Wild yew (*Taxus baccata*) is still extant in the Bristol area, but the yew we are most familiar with is the churchyard yew, which is actually the same species but can look much different. There are yews on the Avon Gorge cliffs and a famous veteran yew in the 200-year-old Parish Wall in Leigh Woods. This yew was old when the wall was built around it. The northern half of Leigh Woods was historically a coppice wood until just 100 years ago; it's now a climax forest of over-mature coppice stools of oak, ash, and small-leafed lime, and lots of understory hazel coppice and rich dead wood. The southern half of Leigh Woods was wood pasture, once part of Ashton Court Estate. A recent survey of the National Nature Reserve (NNR) found 270 old pollard oaks there, 164 still living.

Goblin Combe is still wild yew woodland and also harbours two rare ferns, moonwort fern and limestone fern, as well as stinking hellebore. The ramparts of the hill-fort at Goblin Combe offer one of the most beautiful inland valley vistas of the whole region.

The oldest and arguably the most beautiful yew in Bristol is in the churchyard of Abbots Leigh overlooking a vast view of the Bristol Channel. It is a female yew about 1000 years old and possibly much older. It surely marks the site of an even more ancient cult. Most of the bole is still covered in live wood. Some hollow spaces have been filled with stones, and there's a small arched hollow entrance on the north side. Emblematic of the English countryside, yew groves, yew walks and single yews are associated with many village and

Whitebeam *(Sorbus aria)*.
Leigh Woods

city churchyards, the symbolism in their longevity and their place as gateways between the worlds.

As Bristol botanist White says, 'The propriety of planting in burial places trees so suggestive of silence and gloom has been widely recognized. There is authority also for believing that yew-trees were often planted to protect primitive buildings from wind and storm and likewise to supply good material for longbows and crossbows. It is worthy of note that in many English counties the yew-trees are invariably found on the south side of the churches.' Lutes were also made from yew.

Somerset has many famous yews, one in particular the 3000-year-old yew tree in the churchyard of Ashbrittle near Appley; and another 2000-year-old yew coppice in Silk Wood at Westonbirt Arboretum.

'I never saw a discontented tree. They grip the ground as though they liked it, and though fast rooted they travel about as far as we do. They go wandering forth in all directions with every wind, going and coming like ourselves, traveling with us around the sun two million miles a day, and through space heaven knows how fast and far! We all travel the milky way together, trees and men. Trees are travellers, in the ordinary sense. They make journeys, not very extensive ones, it is true: but our own little comes and goes are only little more than tree-wavings - many of them not so much. '                    **John Muir**

# Saga of the Bristol Whitebeam

Named for the flashing whiteness of its underleaf, whitebeam is cherished by all wayfarers. The Bristol whitebeam (*Sorbus bristoliensis*) is one of the rarest trees in the world and is found only in the Avon Gorge and Leigh Woods. It was first identified by Miss Martha Maria Atwood in 1854 at the overlook at Stokeleigh Camp in Leigh Woods. It's still there. The Bristol whitebeam has sharply lobed leaves and is grey-green underneath, not white like most other whitebeams. There are about 150 of these rare beauty trees across the Gorge.

The Bristol whitebeam is one of eight native trees of the genus Sorbus that are endemic to the Avon Gorge. They are ancient apomictic hybrids, which means that they produce seeds without sex, effectively cloning themselves. The Bristol whitebeam can grow to be a tall tree of 20 metres. It produces creamy white flowers in early summer followed by russet-orange fruits. Specimens can also be seen at the University of Bristol Botanic Garden and at its old site at Bracken Hill across the road from Leigh Woods. The Swedish whitebeam (*Sorbus intermedia*) is a popular street amenity tree in modern England but its wild ancestors still exist in over 50 species.

Tim Rich, one of the experts on the Bristol whitebeam, says one reason why there are so many whitebeams in the Avon Gorge is because the common whitebeam (*Sorbus aria*) cross breeds with every other species available in wind or bird dispersal. 'Probably hundreds of taxa in the gorge have originated in this way, making it a fantastic place for mixing the gene pool. It's the whitebeam equivalent of the mixing of the human gene pool that must have occurred at the height of Bristol's time as a world trading port.'

Although the scientific names have changed, it is worth reading J W White's evocative *Flora of Bristol* entries on the whitebeam and related species. 'Pyrus Aucuparia. Rowan. Mountain-ash. Plentiful near a wood by the Avon above Conham, close to the old Spelter-Works.' Locations in woods near Stapleton, Frenchay, and at the old quarry in Oldbury Park are also mentioned.

> P. Aria. White Beam. Native; in rocky woods, and on naked crags both of limestone and oolite. Occasionally in the Mendip hedges . . . St. Vincent's Rocks, and along the verge of the Avon Gorge. Wyck Rocks. Blaize Castle. Woods above Wotton-under-Edge, in several places. Plentiful in Leigh Woods along the course of the Avon, and on rocks of the valleys that run up from the riverside.

> Pyrus latifolia. Native; in rocky woods; very rare. A very old tree with several boles overhangs some steep rocks on a thickly wood-

ed slope of Clifton Down. Its presence was unsuspected until Sept 1909, and the discovery was due to my finding a sprig with leaf and fruit lying loose on the turf of the 'Green Valley.' Believing it most unlikely to have been brought from the Somerset side of the Avon, I instigated a search through the rocky ground near at hand, and there Miss Roper found this tree. Scrambling boys had been gathering and scattering the berries. Not a single flower could be seen on this tree in 1910, so here again chance has much to do with its discovery in a good fruiting year.

Mr White goes on to describe the discovery of the Bristol whitebeam in the ramparts of Nightingale Valley and the adjacent portion of Leigh Woods by Miss Atwood and first recorded in Swete's *Flora*:

> Growing with P. aria on the summit of Nightingale Valley. For many years these two or three trees were the only ones known in the district. In 1901 the Rev. Augustin Ley wrote me that he had discovered four or five others – some merely coppice bushes, but one fine example of 30 feet or more – some distance to the northward, and the year following I made them out.
>
> P. torminalis. Wild Service-tree. 'Serb' in Sussex, evidently from the old name *Sorb-tree*, in Latin *Sorbus*. Some splendid examples – at least 40 feet high, with boles of four to five feet in girth and clear of branches for some distance above the ground – stand in Chill Wood near Iron Acton, between the railway and the River Frome.

Like hawthorn, whitebeam blossoms can vary enormously from year to year. 'In 1877 the trees on the cliffs of Nightingale Valley flowered splendidly. In the following three seasons there was scarcely a corymb to be seen. . . But in 1881, when every kind of tree flowered most abundantly, the whitebeam seemed to excel them all, and shone forth once more in maximum beauty, the silvery foliage of the older trees being almost hidden by masses of inflorescence.' Most trees have varying flowering and fruiting years, as bee-keepers and cider-makers know.

*Up and down such walks men strolled with rapiers at their sides while our admirals were hammering at the Spanish with culverin and demi-cannon, and looked at the sun-dial and adjourned for a game at bowls, wishing that they only had a chance to bowl shot instead of peaceful wood.*

**Richard Jefferies**, *Trees About Town*

Horse Chestnut
Water Lane, near Temple Quay

Imaginative urban planting inspired
by Bristol Civic Society – Plane trees
(*Platanus x hispanica*)

Ornamental Chinese Maples (*Acer hybrid*)
Temple Meads Gyratory

Following pages:
Coast Redwood *(Sequoia sempervirens)*
and lime trees (Tilia cordata)
Greville Smyth Park

Above: Cut Leaf Beech
*(Fagus sylvatica lacinata)*
Victoria Square, Clifton

Left: Whitebeam *(Sorbus aria)*
Brandon Hill

White's contemporary, the Rev A Ley complained in the early 1900s of the complexities of whitebeam taxonomy: 'I am fain to confess that the relations of these Pyri in the Aria section [the early twentieth-century classification] are terribly intricate, passing the wit of many to disentangle.'

Microspecies even now are treated as species by some botanists and as varieties by others. This is true of many trees and plants in the Kingdoms, Sub-kingdoms, Super-divisions, Divisions, Class, Subclass, Order, Family, Genus, and Species. As Colin Tudge says in his encyclopaedic *The Secret Life of Trees*, 'Modern taxonomy makes some strange bedfellows.'

Names, both common and scientific, will continue changing because of our dedicated and courageous field botanists. Bristol poet, botanist, rock-climber, and whitebeam expert, Libby Houston, has rappelled down the cliffs of the Avon Gorge to botanize and discovered a new hybrid whitebeam, which has since been named after her (*Sorbus x houstoniae*).

# Ghost Tree

The old Huntington elms of Ladies Mile on the Downs are lime trees now. Anyone born after the late 1970s has never seen a mature elm tree, once the emblem of the English countryside. The English elm (*Ulmus procera*) is currently our greatest forest ghost. Its disappearance was caused by a virulent fungal disease the spores of which are carried from tree to tree by bark-beetles, but the lethal agency is a fungus, *Ceratocystis ulmi*. Dutch elm disease, like the old plagues of Europe, has come and gone and come again in vectors of ever more virulent form.

The common name of this disease is unfair to the Dutch; it is indeed a biological heresy to blame a country for the loss of millions of trees. 'Dutch' elm disease got its name because Dutch scientists identified the pathogen after the disease appeared in Holland in 1917. From there it continued to spread, decimating the European elm. From the late 1960s through the 1970s Dutch elm disease killed 10 million mature elms in England alone, dramatically transforming the landscape.

The fungus that causes Dutch elm disease originally came from the Himalayas. It arrived in Europe in the late 1800s; by the 1930s it had spread to North America where it eventually killed most of the elms in the United States and Canada.

The elm will not return to anywhere near its original range in the twenty-first century, but it almost certainly will rise again. Pollen studies show a similar elm die-off in prehistoric times. Although decimated, the English elm is not completely extinct. Elms in hedgerows and forests can still grow into small trees but eventually succumb.

The elms of old appeared in hedges, as pollard groves, as well as large timber trees. The wood was used for everything from buildings to barges and lock gates. The ancient pilings of Bristol Bridge and the Harbour were probably made of elm. Fig, mulberry, hops, cannabis, Osage orange, and nettles are all related to the elm. There have been many elegies to the elm.

The early dawn
The badgers come
And the birds do sing
You were my everything
      Inscription, Ashley Chase Woods

London Plane (*Platanus x hybrida*)

# Ash – The World Tree

*Fraxinus in sylvis pulcherrima*
'The ash is the most beautiful tree in the woods'
**Virgil**

In the United States ash trees are to baseball what willows are to cricket here. The wooden heart of a beloved sport. Ash (*Fraxinus excelsior*) is in the olive family, Oleaceae. Aesc is the Anglo-Saxon for spear. The creamy white timber of ash not only offers the finest firewood (even the green wood burns), but is the favoured wood for oars, billiard cues, hockey sticks, bowling alleys, walking-sticks and ashplants, and the handles of every farm tool for the past 10,000 years. The Fender Telecaster guitar is also made of ash. The incredible lightness of ash extends from the Caucasus Mountains to North America and Asia and is one of the largest of all deciduous trees. The dark maroon flowers of April are male, female, or hermaphrodite, sometimes all on the same tree. There are 80 million ash trees in England. The lovely percentiles say yes, there are more ash trees than there were elms. There are some fine ash trees on the Downs and about one million others in our surrounding woods and forests.

Ash is the sacred World Tree, Yggdrasil, in the Norse epic *The Poetic Edda* and in *The Prose Edda* of Snorri Sturluson. Ash, after thorn, is the most common place-name in England since Anglo-Saxon times. Although ash is not the longest lived tree of the forest, 200 years at most, there are coppiced stands hundreds of years older.

The new ash plague sounds like a demon from an unknown forest epic. The Chalara fraxinea fungus seems to have originated in Japan or Korea but the Asian fungus does not affect the local Manchurian ash trees there. One tree's pathogen is another's harmless bug. Although reported in Eastern Europe 20 years ago, it was discovered in Denmark in 2002, and within a few years the disease had spread across

Above: Regent Street, Clifton
Decades to grow, gone in just a few minutes
– tree surgeons in action.

Opposite: The stumps of plane trees on Clarence
Road, Redcliffe. They are retained to preserve the
tree pit to enable replacement planting.

the country. Today 95% of ash trees in Denmark are dead or dying. Very few ash trees seem to have a natural resistance to the fungus.

Prof. Erik Kjaer, of the University of Copenhagen, speaking to the BBC said, 'It is a terrible disease and this is the only kind of optimism I can offer the UK: there seems to be some kind of resistance and maybe it can work. But of course this is based on a very pessimistic view that the vast majority of trees seem to be highly susceptible.' The future of the ash will be a long process of botanomancy, forest research, cellular science, and hard grafting.

In hindsight, this quote from White is a little foreboding: 'If elm heads the list, the ash must come next among the commonest trees of our hedgerows. There are plenty of natural ash woods among the limestone hills about Bristol. On Mendip many of the woods are truly primitive: relics doubtless of the historic Saxon hunting forest, where in all probability the ash was always the most abundant tree.'

The beauty of ash in an Avon Gorge-like setting is well described by the painter and engraver Jacob George Strutt in his *Sylva Britannica*:

> It is in mountain scenery that the ash appears to particular advantage; waving its slender branches over some precipice which just affords it soil sufficient for its footing, or springing between crevices of rock, a happy emblem of the hardy spirit which will not be subdued by fortune's scantiness. It is likewise a lovely object by the side of some crystal stream. In which it views its elegant pendent foliage, bending, Narcissus-like, over its own charms.

In Barry Cunliffe's book, *Britain Begins*, there is a photograph of the archaeological excavations at the Star Carr mesolithic site, near Scarborough, dated to about 9000 BC which clearly shows the full trunk of a preserved ash tree. The tree was at least 100 years old when felled by our ancestors.

There is no easy way to say this, but the ash tree fungus, as horrifying as it sounds, is not our only forest problem. In France another fungus is affecting the Canal du Midi plane trees. The great iconic trees of the

Dead wood – a feast for many species
Leigh Woods

south which van Gogh painted are now dead or dying and are being cut down. These colannades of the French rivers and canals are said to have been originally infected from the wood of ammunition cases or packing material brought from America during World War II. In this case a North America fungus from the American sycamore? There are other threats. Sudden Oak Death, first identified in northern California, has killed thousands of oaks throughout the state and has also been identified here.

As we noted earlier, anyone born after 1970 will have no memory of the English elm. In the same way, our grandchildren and their children may be unfamiliar with the English ash. But what's happening to our global canopy may just be an ancient cycle: die-back, plague, extinction, rebirth. The forest has done this many times before.

On 16 October 1987 a great storm felled some 15 million trees in England. In 1990 another hurricane swept southern England. Many forests and woods were obliterated, thousands of huge Legacy trees lost. A landscape changed overnight. There was great sorrow. I know this horror. On 11 September 1992 I was living in Hawai'i when Hurricane Iniki, a Category 4 storm, devastated the forests and homes of the Garden Isle of Kaua'i. A quarter century later the damage is hard to see on any of these islands. The word for forest is regeneration.

## The Secret Forests of Bristol

(Not a list but a chant. Deliberately omitted are most parks, plantations, and nature reserves. Walkers and map readers will recognize a discontinuous forest trail beginning in the north and following a boustrophedon path from west to east and back again in a southerly progression.)

Monmouth Covert, Catbrain Wood, Pegwell Wood, Round Covert, Woodlands Wood, Spaniorum, Savage's Wood, Webb's Wood, Ball Wood, Urchin Wood, Lower Woods, Hawkesbury Common, Inglestone Common, North Elms Wood, South Elms Wood, Stiff's Coppice, Sturt

Coppice, Oakhill Coppice, Spoil Coppice, Lance Coppice, Lower Wetmoor Wood, Bishop's Hill Wood, Mossy Wood, Littley Wood, Burnt Wood, Sturgeon Wood, Bays Wood, Stonybridge Wood, Lady's Wood, Withymore Wood, Hortham Wood, Cat Grove, Roundhouse Wood, Swift's Wood, Daniel's Wood, Michael Wood, Furzeground Wood, Iron Mill Grove, Kington Grove, Cassey Grove, Filnor Woods, Backwell Hill Woods, The Island, Norton's Wood, Rock Wood, Simshill Wood, Sandford Wood, Chummock Wood, Dunhill Wood, Cockheap Wood, Cleeve Toot, Wrington Warren, Goblin Combe, Spying Copse, Hanging Wood, Round Wood, Old Withy Bed, Chill Wood, Haw Wood, Berwick Wood, Moorgrove Wood, Bangley Wood, Hollyhill Wood, Chandler's Brake, Hakes Hill Wood, South Hill Wood, Sherbourne's Brake, Rockwell Wood, Blackberry Brake, Hotwater Brake, Burn Wood, Ramhill Wood, Martin Croft Brake, Branch Pool Wood, Idover Wood, Lyegrove Wood, Frenchpiece Wood, Dodington Wood, Overscourt Wood, Tut's Wood, Primrose Wood, Warmley Forest Park, Bottom Hill Wood, Gunnin's Wood, Harcombe Wood, Dunsdown Beeches, Clifton Wood, St John's Wood, Cloud Wood, Marshfield Wood, Raizes Wood, Clift Wood, Cherry Wood, Diamond Wood, Monk Woods, Longley Wood, Blackhorse Wood, Fenn's Wood, Hammerhill Wood, Whistley Wood, Great Wood, Bitham's Wood, Catsley Wood, Pepper Shells, Wooscombe Wood, Lord's Wood, Publow Wood, Cockroad Wood, Whidcombe Brake, Poacher's Pocket, Dowling's Wood, Curl's Wood, Atgrove Wood, Glebe Wood, Stantonbury Hill, West Wood, Middle Wood, Whistling Copse, Cabot's Wood, Ash Wood, Dressnell's Wood, Taylor's Wood, Green's Wood, Prestow Wood, Shippenhay Wood, Little Horts Wood, Horts Wood, Barley Wood, Tucker's Grove, Whitley Coppice, Bottenham Coppice, Dead Hill Wood, Slade Wood, Batches Wood, Martin's Wood, Steven's Wood, Nipper's Copse, Chelvey Wood, Breach Hill Wood, Hyatt's Wood, Oatfield Wood, Park Wood, Dog Kennel Wood, Vernham Wood, Pipley Wood, Beach Wood, Rushmead Wood, Ashcombe Wood, Hunterwick Wood, Summerhill Wood, Cherrywell Wood, Dicknick Wood, Bandywell Wood, Cowleaze Wood, Stillcombe Wood, Bailey's Wood, Short Wood, Bean Wood, Wapley Bushes, Ham Wood, East Wood, Penpole Wood,

Crabtree Slip Wood, Thirty Acre Wood, Evergreens Wood, Blaise Castle Estate, Limekiln Wood, Goram's Chair, Three Acre Covert, Southside Wood, Alderdown Wood, Sheep Wood, Badocks Wood, Splatts Abbey Wood, Long Wood, Hermitage Wood, Barn Wood, Pond Field Wood, Oldbury Court Estate, Snuff Mills, Frenchay Mill, Lincombe Barn Woods, Weston Wood, Seven Acre Wood, Weston Big Wood, West Wood, Barrow Wood, Prior's Wood, Birch Wood, Bullings Wood, Longlands Wood, Hail's Wood, Budding's Wood, Breach Wood, Durban's Batch, Alder Bed Wood, West Tanpit Wood, East Tanpit Wood, Three Cornered Wood, Snakes Well Wood, Fish Pond Wood, Jubb's Wood, Leigh Wood, The Folly, Black Moor Wood, Old Park Wood, Leigh Court, Paradise Bottom, Oak Wood, Sea Mills Wood, Leigh Woods, Durdham Down, Watcombe Slade, Clifton Down, Fifty Acre Wood, Church Wood, Brandon Hill, St Anne's Wood, Burrington Combe, Rowberrow Warren, Dolebury Warren, Fen's Wood, Keed's Wood, Hanging Hill Wood, Barrow Wood, Charcoal Wood, Bowman's Wood, Ridings Wood, High Wood, Common Wood, Barrow Big Wood, Manor Wood, The Malago, East Wood, Fox's Wood, Hencliff Wood, Dundridge Farm Woods, Bickley Wood, Cleeve Wood, Abbotts Wood, Manor Road Community Wood, Foxhall Wood, Weston Wood, Kelston Round Hill, Shagbear Wood, Tennant's Wood, Brown's Folly, Cleaves Wood, Chapel Wood, Aldermoor Wood, Folly Wood.

The Bristol Community Forest Path follows an inner circle of these woods for 45 miles through Bristol and environs.

*How vainly men themselves amaze*
*To win the palm, the oak, or bays,*
*And their uncessent labours see*
*Crowned from some single herb or tree,*
*Whose short and narrow-vergèd shade*
*Does prudently their toils upbraid;*
*While all flowers and all trees do close*
*To weave the garlands of repose!*
**Andrew Marvell**

London Plane *(Platanus x Europaea)*
St John's Road, Clifton

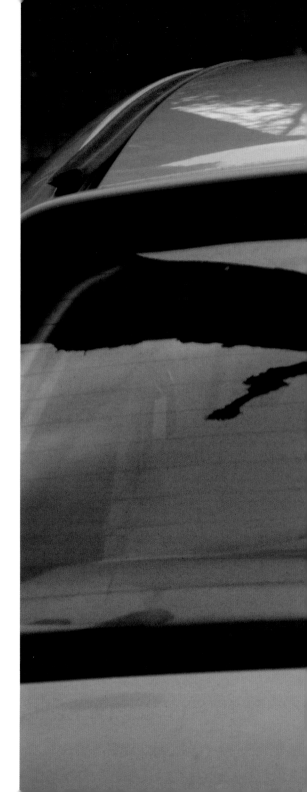

# Lime Tree Bower

Although not actually in Bristol, mention must be made of Shervage Wood, Coleridge's forest in the Quantocks, the forest of inspiration that led directly to the publication of the first book in the Romantic Movement. *Lyrical Ballads* by William Wordsworth and Samuel T Coleridge was published by Joseph Cottle in Wine Street, Bristol in 1798. Not far from Nether Stowey, near Porlock Weir, are the petrified remains of a submerged forest visible at low tides.

> The roaring dell, o'erwooded, narrow, deep,
> And only speckled by the mid-day Sun;
> Where its slim trunk the Ash from rock to rock
> Flings arching like a Bridge; that branchless Ash,
> Unsunned and damp, whose few poor yellowed leaves
> Ne'er tremble in the gale, yet tremble still,
> Fann'd by the waterfall!
> > **Samuel T Coleridge**
> > 'This Lime-Tree Bower My Prison'

In Roman times the small-leafed lime was known as the tree of a thousand uses: rope, nets, clothing, most farm and household tools, and fuel. There is a great ancient lime in Leigh Woods over 250 years old. The small-leaved lime (*Tilia cordata*) is the truly ancient woodland tree of England. Westonbirt Arboretum's 2000-year-old small-leaf lime, a huge coppice stool forming a small copse in itself, is coppiced every 30 years – an ancient forest management practice now well recognized as most sustainable.

The name cordata is from the Latin *cordatus* for the lime tree's heart-shaped leaves. Lime is the Old English word for tree, lind; in Germany, the linde, or linden tree. The small-leafed lime, or pry tree, is not the common lime, the large leaf variety planted in city parks. Limes outside their native woods become very social trees, their crowns forming fine domes when planted in rows of avenues, one of the finest in Bristol at Temple Park behind the leaning Temple Church.

*In drear-nighted December*
*Too happy, happy tree,*
*Thy branches ne'er remember*
*Their green felicity:*
*The north cannot undo them,*
*With a sleety whistle through them;*
*Nor frozen thawings glue them*
*From budding at the prime.*

> **John Keats**

Brandon Hill

Hawthorn *(Crategus monogyna)*.
Brandon Hill

# The Mays of Bristol

Summer is y-comen in,
Loudė sing, cuckoo!

**Anon**

'May. Hawthorn. Whitethorn. *(Crataegus monogyna)*. Hawthorn sometimes appear as if in clumps, their bodies divided and multiplied, which is a sign of extreme old age. The wildly grotesque features of ancient olive-trees have probably been acquired by a similar, if more lengthy, process. Olive-yards exist, at least in Majorca, with a known history of close upon a thousand years, and trees so old have naturally developed eccentricities more pronounced than any we may see among our hawthorns.'

'The 'Holy Thorn' of Glastonbury which, according to legend, sprang from the staff of Joseph of Arimathea when a missionary in Britain, was for centuries an object of veneration and pilgrimage. It has the singular habit of often blooming a second time about Christmas-tide. This habit is shared by its descendants, raised from seed or cuttings, that have been well distributed. One of these stands amid the abbey ruins; another in the garden of All Saints, Clifton.'

Our botanist White also identifies a strange may on the Downs near Sea Walls bearing attractive, apple-like fruit. Avalon haws? Many English botanists over the centuries, including Turner, Gerard and Parkinson, have commented on this hawthorn (whether it be a separate species or not).

> In a favourable season when bloom is profuse the view to be had from the Observatory Hill, looking northward over our Downs dotted with masses of pearl and silver, will yield to few in beauty. The praise of such a scene has been sung by almost every poet, scarcely one omitting to take up the theme of the fragrant May.

Copper beech (*Fagus sylvatica f. purpurea*)
Park Place, Clifton

In deep summer all Bristol becomes the woods. In autumn the trees wear see-through leaves like punk ballerinas in torn tutus. In winter the Bristol skyline is a surrealist ambush of chimneys and urban pollard trees, the unpruned balls like black sea urchins against the sky. But spring, spring is the promise. The may is the flower of the troubadours and Beltane, the good time of the year.

As Virgil says, may the forest be your song.

Following pages:
Common Lime, Goldney Road, Clifton

P110-111: Ashton Court Estate

## Select Bibliography

William Anderson and Clive Hicks. *Green Man*. HarperCollins. London and San Francisco. 1990.

Gaston Bachelard. *The Poetics of Reverie*. Grossman. 1969.

Christopher Bloor. *Crossing Boundaries: The Community Forest Path*. Closer To The Countryside Books. 2007.

Peter Bogdanovich. *A Year and a Day Calendar*. The Overlook Press. 1990.

*Book of the British Countryside*. AA, Drive Publications. 1973.

Eugene Byrne and Simon Gurr. *The Bristol Story*. Bristol Cultural Development Partnership. 2007.

Barry Cunliffe. *Britain Begins*. Oxford University Press. 2013.

Roger Deakin. *Wildwood, A Journey Through Trees*. Penguin. 2007.

Rosalind Delany, Gillian Winn. *How Did This Garden Grow – The History of the Botanic Gardens of the University of Bristol*. The Friends of Bristol University Botanic Garden. 2002.

John Fowles. *The Tree*. Little, Brown 1979. Ecco Press 2010.

Robert Graves. *The White Goddess*. International Authors. 1948.

Francis Greenacre. *From Bristol To The Sea*. Redcliffe Press. 2005.

Robert Pogue Harrison. *Forests, The Shadow of Civilization*. University of Chicago Press. 1992.

Ronald Hutton. *Blood and Mistletoe: The History of the Druids in Britain*. Yale University Press. 2009.

Anna Lewington and Edward Parker. *Ancient Trees*. Collins & Brown. London. 1999.

C M Lovatt, Libby Houston, L C Frost. *The Nationally Scarce Plants of the Avon Gorge and Its Environs*. University of Bristol Avon Gorge Project. Report No. 17. 1993.

William Bryant Logan. *Oak, The Frame of Civilization*. Norton. 2005.

Richard Mabey. *Beechcombings*. Chatto and Windus. 2007.

Marion Mako. *The University of Bristol Gardens*. University of Bristol. 2011.

Archie Miles. *The Trees That Made Britain*. BBC Books. 2006.

J Edward Milner. *The Tree Book*. Collins and Brown. 1992.

Sarah L Myles, Editor. *The Flora of the Bristol Region*. Bristol Regional Environmental Records Centre. 2000.

Adele Nozedar. *The Hedgerow Handbook*. Square Peg. 2012.

Oldbury Court Primary School, et al. *The Forgotten Estate*. Acta Community Theatre. 2004.

Jacqueline Memory Paterson. *Tree Wisdom*. Thorsons. 1996.

Oliver Rackham. *Woodlands*. Collins. 2010.

W L Rew. *Memories of Wraxall*. Nailsea and District Local Historical Society. 1981.

Tim Rich, Libby Houston, Ashley Robertson, Michael Proctor. *Whitebeams, Rowans and Service Trees of Britain and Ireland*. Botanical Society of the British Isles. 2010.

James Russell. *The Naked Guide To Cider*. Tangent Books. Bristol. 2010.

John Shaw. *Tree Hunting and Walking in North Somerset*. Woodspring, Weston-super-Mare. 2004.

Jon Stokes, Donald Rodger. *The Heritage Trees of Britain & Northern Ireland*. Photographs by Archie Miles and Edward Parker. Constable, London. 2004.

Geraldine Taylor. *The Bristol Downs*. Broadcast Books. 2008.

Edward Thomas. *The South Country*. London. 1909.

Graham Tissington. *Long Ashton*. Bristol. 1966.

Colin Tudge. *The Secret Life of Trees*. Allen Lane. 2005.

Giambattista Vico. *The New Science*. Cornell University Press. 1968.

Alfred Watkins. *The Old Straight Track*. 1925.

*Watsonia. Journal of the Botanical Society of the British Isles*. February 2009.

John White. *Forest and Woodland Trees in Britain*. Oxford University Press. 1995.

John Walton White. *The Flora of Bristol*. John Wright and Sons. Bristol. 1912.

Katie White and Roy Gallop, Editors. *A Celebration of the Avon New Cut*. Fiducia Press. 2006.

Herbert S Zim and Alexander C Martin. *Trees*. Golden Press, New York. 1961.

Websites can be more ephemeral than printed books but here's one that's lasted:

Ancient Trees International at www.ancientforests.org.

Also: www.treeregister.org has a large yew collection compiled by the Ancient Yew Group, and www.ancient-tree-hunt.org.uk is the ongoing archive of ancient and legacy trees.

## Frank Drake

Frank Drake born/brought up in NW London.
Education commenced after leaving school at 14,
when he retired shortly afterwards. Travelled/worked
extensively throughout Europe, West Africa, India
and the US, including Paris, Istanbul, Athens, Toronto
and San Francisco. Started Bristol's cinema club
'The Filmpit'; BA, UWE (Fine Art in Context);
MA: 'The Willing Suspension of Disbelief' (ongoing);
Photographer for WOMAD – *Sounds of Music*
published by Tangent Books; *Advanced Portrait
Photography* (collaboration) Blandford Press; the first
graffiti exhibition, Arnolfini; and *The Pyramid* – a
substantial sculpture representing free speech and
sustainability, to be erected in Belfast 2015. Currently
working on 'Bristol's (Britain's) Moveable Forest',
(www.b-m-f.org).

## Tony D'Arpino

Tony D'Arpino was born in Mount Holly, New
Jersey. His first book of poetry was entitled *The
Tree Worshipper*. Other books include *The Shape of
The Stone*, *Seven Dials*, *Greatest Hits*, and *Floating
Harbour* (Redcliffe Press). For a number of years he
managed a forest reserve on the Big Island of Hawai'i.
He has worked as an actor, book reviewer, charity
development director, theatre producer, and trade
show installer. He has been a Djerassi fellow and has
lived in San Francisco, Hawai'i and Europe. His poem
'Pero's Bridge', appears in the anthology *The Echoing
Gallery: Bristol Poets and Art in the City*, published
by Redcliffe Press.